Never Again!

Ten Years of Hitler

A SYMPOSIUM

Edited by

STEPHEN S. WISE

Published by

JEWISH OPINION PUBLISHING CORPORATION

19 WEST 44TH STREET, NEW YORK

1943

TABLE OF CONTENTS

5

TABLE OF CONTENTS

Hitlerism—And Beyond

A FOREWORD

Opinion has justified pride in the symposium which it presented to its readers on the subject, "Ten Years of Hitler." Contributors to this symposium are a company of eminent Americans, eminent in many fields of life and its endeavors. Opinion is so sure of the permanent value of the contributions to this symposium, that it has made arrangement for the publication in volume form of the following series of articles from the pen of men and women who understand the evil of Hitlerism, many of whom have long deplored it, and all of whom recognize that the Dark Decade, or the Decade of Death, must become the precursor to a new and gladder day for mankind.

What better summary of the immeasurable evil that has been wrought throughout these awful ten years than the word, "There is not an evil in humanity which has not been worsened, and not a good that has not been weakened during these ten years of Hitler's rule." The former half of the statement is indubitably true. The second half may be challenged from the viewpoint of those who believe that the worst has already been, that thanks to the incredible effort and the unwithstandable unity of the Allied Nations, Hitlerism is to be driven from the face of the earth.

True enough, alas, good has been weakened, and it was the weakening of the good which made possible the tragic toleration of Hitlerism by those nations which ultimately found it necessary to withstand the illimitable evil that lies at its heart. Many of the best and most precious things of life have been assailed and for a time overcome, but it is not too much to say that the light is beginning to dawn, even for the most reluctant of them that finally came to resist Hitlerism. Now it is clear to all who see, who are not willfully blind, that an unresisted Hitlerism would have meant the destruction—it might have been for centuries, if not millenia—of every value for which men of faith and courage and aspiration have wrought and fought throughout the ages. May it not truly be said that for a time, when Hitler began to rage, there was a woeful toleration of the evil that he meant to those who would not understand. After the years of toleration and compromise a great dread rested upon individuals and peoples, lest the world succumb to or be overwhelmed by the threatening evil. Today, however, that is, alas, only after a decade of easy tolerance or of explicable dread, the world of freemen has put aside alike its tolerance and its dread, substituting for these things the will to achieve victory as against every power of enslavement and degradation menacing mankind. Even better, the wisest and the finest within the leadership of the nations will not rest satisfied merely to overcome the evil that confronted them. They are, in the word of one of the truest builders of the democratic faith of our own country, "resolved to build a better world, a world of peaceful work, in which the millions still living can be free from haunting fear and can play their part as citizens in a new and universal democracy."

For ten years OPINION has published a symposium comparable with that which distinguishes its Tenth

8

Commemoration Issue. It had been believed that the scourge would be stayed within a brief period. Therein it has been disappointed, for ten years unutterably bitter and unprecedentedly tragic have passed since Hindenburg and Von Papen awarded the crown of leadership to Hitler. For the first time since Hitler's coming, there is good hope of his going. The free and democratic peoples are united, and no power under heaven can hold their resistless march. As has been their lot throughout the ages, Jews have been the earliest and the greatest sufferers. Even this price which Jews have paid will not be accounted too great if the downfall of Hitler and the whole miserable Nazi-Fascist company will come to mean as it should, that if ever again an anti-Jewish movement be initiated, it and his authors will be suspect wheresoever they might dwell. Anti-Semitism becomes even more intolerable within our borders than within the frontiers of a nation that has not striven to accept the democratic way of life.

The century of the common man, without regard to creed or race or color, is at hand. As Jews we have borne the heaviest burden. We have faith that humankind will recognize as never before that Jews have become the victims of the Fascist terrorism because they are the unbowed protagonists of freedom, faith, democracy. The nations must be united in safeguarding the four freedoms for all men and peoples. The Jew today looks forward to a new world for all men, including himself. The Jew has always made his own permanent contribution to the upbuilding of a moral world. Freedom and equality for the Jew will liberate and inspire the Jew to renew his gifts and to redouble his service for the weal of all mankind.

—*Stephen S. Wise*

That Freedom May Be Reborn

By Henry A. Wallace
Vice President of the United States

For ten years the world has been torn by a desperate struggle between two opposite forces. One force, destructive, was typified by the barbarous and unspeakable cruelties practiced by the Nazis under Hitler and by the militarists of Japan. The other force, constructive, was typified by the humane movements in the United States and elsewhere, the goal of which was to better the lot of mankind. One force stood for human slavery. The other stood for human freedom.

These two forces could not live side by side in the world indefinitely. One or the other was bound to gain the ascendancy. In this war they have come to grips on the battlefield, and the struggle is being fought out to a decision.

In this struggle, millions are paying with their lives in order that freedom in the world may be reborn. We can not bring those millions back to life. But we can dedicate ourselves to the great task of building a better world—a world of peaceful work—in which the millions still living can be free from haunting fear and can play their part as citizens in a new and universal democracy.

Every racial group will be needed in this great task. Each, through its own culture, its own genetic heritage, can make its own peculiar contribution. The democracy we hope to see will be a combination of them all.

To Free Mankind

By Cordell Hull

United States Secretary of State

This country was shocked and outraged, when tyranny and barbarity again commenced their march, at the brutality which was inflicted on certain races, and particularly on the Jewish populations of Europe. Apparently no form of abuse has been too great, and no form of torture or oppression too vile, to be meted out to these populations by the Nazi despots. And, in taking this attitude towards the Jewish race, they have made it plain by concrete acts that a like attitude would be taken towards any other race against whom they might invent a grievance.

The Jews have long sought a refuge. I believe that we must have an even wider objective; we must have a world in which Jews, like every other race, are free to abide in peace and in honor.

Today the battle for freedom is being carried on in the East and in the West and our every effort is concentrated on a successful issue. We can with confidence look forward to the victory when liberty shall lift the scourge of persecution and the might of the United Nations free mankind from the threat of oppression.

Of all the inhuman and tyrannical acts of Hitler and

his Nazi lieutenants, their systematic persecution of the Jewish people—men, women and children—is the most debased. The fate of these unhappy people must be ever before us in the efforts we are making today for the final victory; at the moment of triumph under the terms of the Atlantic Charter the United Nations will be prepared not only to redeem their hopes of a future world based upon freedom, equality and justice but to create a world in which such a tragedy will not again occur.

War's Worst Horror

By Francis Biddle

Attorney General of the United States

PERSECUTION of minorities is not new—persecution because of race, because of color, because of creed. Throughout the sad pages of history men have ruthlessly tortured and exterminated human beings who differed, who would not conform, who clung to their own gods. But as the world grew, as education and religion spread, and the seeds of democracy took root, a consciousness that human nature was, after all, of the same flesh and blood and spirit, drew men's hearts to resist oppression, to hate persecution. In America we declared that all men were created free and equal, and later forbade discrimination on account of race and color.

Each religious group had taken its turn in suffering from the hands of society—the early Christians, the Protestants against the Catholic States, the Catholics when they were in the minority, the Quakers, and throughout the world and over long periods of time, the Jews, who were so often scattered and helpless against the cruelty of dominant power.

In time tolerance spread, and the Christian idea prevailed; there was hope for oppressed people, for the little national and racial minorities. Human beings were learning that they could live and let live.

But that change was halted ten years ago in Germany. Under the new teaching Germans must learn to hate. Hitler had learned to hate, so too should his people be taught. What better victims than the Jews? Hatred could unite a people, cruelty could make them strong. But the job must be thorough, scientific, educational. So he set about the studied process of suppression as a national and patriotic program. The Jews would be declared untouchables, barred from the professions, segregated. The Nazi regime responded, and the program broadened. If the Jews were a menace to Hitler's power so too were Protestants and Catholics, labor leaders, scientists, writers—all free men who believed that truth was more important than this naive yet obscene worship of the beast. And then the swift conquest of Poland and the rest of unhappy Europe, and the starving and tortured and slain victims of the idea of racial superiority.

This is the worst horror of the war, this resurgence on a vast scale of the ancient persecutions, the use of cruelty as state policy, of starvation and torture as legal process. For it plunges the people whose system it is back into the barbarous world from which, we had once thought, humanity had escaped.

Humanity has not escaped. Humanity will not escape till we, the United Nations, fighting everywhere for restoration of a decent tolerance, purge the world of this wretched, this archaic horror.

The Day of Deliverance
By Bishop William T. Manning

T HE Nazi assault upon the Jews, and their attempt thus to exterminate a whole people, is a crime so diabolical, so inhuman, so utterly cruel and wicked, that no language can describe it. Those who are carrying out the orders of Hitler are the enemies of Civilization, of Human Decency, and of every principle of Christianity, and at the centre of their crimes stands their assault upon the Jewish People. For the sake of mankind this Evil Power must be crushed and destroyed. May we in America do everything in our power to hasten the day when our Jewish brethren in Europe shall be delivered from these oppressors, when the guilty leaders shall be brought to the Bar of Justice, and Victory for Right and Freedom shall open the way for a Fellowship of Nations which shall bring a truer World Order and lasting Peace.

Moral Monstrosity

By Rt. Rev. Monsignor John A. Ryan
Director National Catholic Welfare
Conference

THE enormous cruelties inflicted upon the Jewish
people of Germany ought to move every Christian
heart to pity, ought to prevent any Christian from
doing and saying anything which would mock their
sufferings, outrage their sensibilities and make their lot
harder to bear. This involves Jews everywhere—even
those who are our fellow citizens in the United States.

In order to find enemies of the human race comparable with this moral monstrosity (Hitler) one has to go
back to the fifth century Hun, Attila, who came to be
called "the Scourge of God," or to the twelfth century
Mongol, Genghis Khan, who believed that he had a
divine call to conquer the world. And Hitler's capacity
for evil is greater than was that of either of those ter-
rifying and devastating barbarians.

The Culmination of Barbarism

By Thomas E. Dewey
Governor of New York

As we enter the second year of war with the Axis we recognize more than ever the deep-seated and universal nature of the attack on our civilization by Hitlerism. The barbarism, always implicit in the movement, now reaches its culmination as the forces of the Axis reel from the offensives by the United Nations on the different fronts.

Starting with discrimination, then segregation and the humiliation of individuals, and following through with the suppression and destruction of many human beings, it has now bared its purpose to destroy every standard of conduct that has distinguished mankind from the beast. This is the significance of the attempt to exterminate whole peoples on the continent of Europe upon which attempt the Nazis are now engaged. No longer is an effort made to justify or explain on the ground of specific circumstances or specific conditions. Now only the total extermination of whole peoples will satisfy the sadism of the followers of Hitler.

This very outburst, however, may well be partly caused by the Nazi recognition that the long held initiative has been lost. It is further proof that our enemies know they cannot exist so long as there is a free world to fight them. It fortifies the more our determination and that of our Allies that a complete and crushing victory must be the only object of our effort. We have now, for more than a year been a united people, resolved to a single decision. These new atrocities will only serve to arouse further the revulsion and determination of every American, once for all, to wipe the forces of cruelty and atavism from the earth.

A Day of Reckoning

By F. H. La Guardia
Mayor of New York

THE month of February, 1943, marks the tenth year of Hitlerism. It is our fervent prayer that it will also mark the last year of this degraded philosophy based on brutality and crime.

A careful study of world history reveals no more bestial reign of terror and inhumanity than that now practiced by Hitler and his cohorts. The Nazis have sunk to an all-time low in the annals of human behavior. Sadism and Nazism are synonymous. These mad dogs of Europe find actual pleasure in inflicting pain and in watching their victims suffer. The relentless slaughter of Jews in Poland is a horrible nightmare. Innocent men, women and children are left to die slowly from starvation or they are suddenly dragged from their pestilence-ridden ghettos and murdered. They have no choice but death. Death is their salvation. Death is their only hope of escape from pain, from prolonged suffering, from dread disease.

Day by day, we, the United Nations, come one step nearer to putting these atrocities to an end. Day by day, we the United Nations, renew our solemn oath that these murders will be avenged. This blood has not been shed in vain. These murderers will face a day of reckoning.

The Last Anniversary!

By William Green

President, American Federation of Labor

AMERICAN labor is resolved that this tenth anniversary of Hitlerism shall be the last.

The Nazi record of the past decade has been a record of progress—in infamy. Born in violence, Nazism showed its evil character during its infancy when it espoused and practiced persecution of the Jews. The growth of its criminal career, marked by the enslavement of labor, the suppression of all freedoms, the stifling of religion and the degradation of human beings into serfs of the State, has now culminated in a total war against the free peoples of the world.

Because this war was forced upon us, it is often said that it was none of our making, that we were not in any way responsible. But, in a broad sense, our country and the other free nations were responsible for permitting the growth of Nazi terrorism to continue unchecked, for blinding ourselves to the reality that tyranny and oppression, even when far removed from our own shores, will eventually strike at us.

Now that we have enlisted all our human and physical resources in the battle to destroy Hitlerism, we know that we will not be secure unless victory brings full assurance that the forces of intolerance, hate and violence will never again be allowed to flourish on the face of the earth.

To that end we dedicate our sufferings and our sacrifices and all our efforts.

History's Worst Record

By Pearl S. Buck

T EN years of Hitler rule have now unrolled themselves. The record is the worst the world's history has ever known. It is a solemn thing to contemplate the evils for which one man can be responsible to so large a degree. Millions of people are dead, race hatred has been so deepened that it may take generations longer to wipe it out, starvation has been visited upon peoples to an extent never before reached, murder has been called morality, the home has been desecrated in the name of a false patriotism, women have been degraded and children held as no better than animals to be bred for the glory of the owner state. There is not an evil in humanity which has not been worsened, and not a good which has not been weakened during these ten years of Hitler's rule.

And yet there is profound reason for hope. The wickedness of one man who crept into power has made all men and women aware as never before of the necessity for individual goodness and morality. Machinery extends today the power of the individual, and it is essential for the welfare of all that the individual must be better, more human, more intelligent, more moral, than ever before. The power of a bad man is too dangerous. We must have goodness.

Goodness must be the foundation of human life. The

goodness of human equality, of freedom of peoples, of kindness and cooperation, upon goodness human society must be built as the only practical way of making life endurable. The honor of the individual must be restored, so that individual honesty is valued again, and the honor of nations must be restored so that a promise can hold. It is impossible to accomplish and to achieve when men lie and nations break their word. There is no structure of life possible unless it can be built upon mutual trust and honor.

Yes, Hitler has done this—he has shown us within a brief span of years how horrible evil can be when it is unloosed to full power. He has made all the peoples of the world long as they have never longed for righteousness and for the beauty of goodness. Surely there are those even among his own people who share this longing of the world.

The Cleansing Force

By James P. Pope

Director, Tennessee Valley Authority

For ten years, Nazism has been on demonstration to the world. Its philosophy has been propounded in words and action. There is no longer a reason for any one not to know what it is and what kind of world it proposes.

What is called Nazism today has known many ages, many lands, and many names. It has expressed itself in ignorance and hatred of class toward class, religion toward religion, race toward race, nation toward nation; in economic peonage, in lynching and gangster mob rule, in relics of feudalism and superstition, in spiritual poverty and hopelessness. They have been the lapses, the points of failure, of societies.

It remained for Nazism to gather up the most shameful failings of the world's societies and to combine them into a system of despotism animated by hatred. In the resulting degradation of a once-great people we can see our own and our neighbors' shortcomings, made the rule rather than the exception, grotesquely magnified and distorted.

If we truly know what it is that we see, if we know Nazism for what it plainly is, ours may be the cleansing force of a disgust stronger and more adamant than any other generation has ever known. With it we may not only rid the world of the shame that darkens Germany, Japan, and Italy; we may also clear away the vestiges of darkness that lie upon our own lands and our own hearts.

Tragic Justice Looms Ahead

By Paul V. McNutt
Chairman, War Manpower Commission

For ten years the bestiality of Nazism has been in power. These have been ten years of loathsome oppression, of mounting power. From the persecution of the Jew the Nazis have gone on to other crimes. Labor has been enslaved, womanhood degraded, religion destroyed. And for over three years a savage war of destruction has been waged against the free peoples of the earth. But now, at long last, full circle approaches. A dramatic and tragic justice looms before us. For at this moment a horribly intensified, mammoth persecution of the Jewish people—an attempt at actual mass extermination—tells us that this foulest tyranny in history is desperately conscious of its own approaching doom. Once again, as often before in the long centuries of Jewish history, the time is at hand when out of the ashes of persecution will flower anew the doctrines of liberal thought which have linked the Jews and other civilized peoples since time began.

But this time, we citizens of the United Nations, peoples of all faiths, are determined that the word "civilized" shall mean something more than it has in the past. Never before has the spirit of man cried out so loudly as today against aggression and injustice, against everything that has made possible the horror of the past ten years. We are determined to strike down for ever, beyond the possibility of ever rising again, the evil that has been the cause of this great tragedy of our modern world.

The pattern of this new justice, of this new civilization, begins to emerge. In our determination we are achieving unprecedented unity not only among nations but also within our borders. Here at home in the United States, we see with exultation that every day more of our people realize that our fighting men do not ask the race or creed or color of the men and women who make their guns. Our democracy is on the march by the side of its allies.

The Nazis have attempted to kill ideas and ideals by killing men and women who have held them. But we know that this is a delusion—that ideas die only when hope dies. And the tragedy of the Jewish people in Europe fans to an ever fiercer intensity the hope and the determination of all men of free spirit.

The Scourge is Passing

By Newbold Morris

TEN years of Hitler! This thought strikes us forcibly. How is it possible that a pestilence could endure so long? Many were those who thought that the virus could be isolated; that those who became infected with it could be quarantined. Many were those who hoped that it was not strong enough to persist; that it would gradually evaporate in the soft zephyr-like breeze of humanitarism.

During those ten years we have found that there is no doubt of the persistence of this infection. That those who seek to indoctrinate the cynical and take advantage of the complacent must be destroyed utterly, unequivocally and finally.

Once having made up their minds on this point, the people of the United Nations have acquired a grim determination and a will for destruction, which is not ordinarily associated with the democratic way of life. This toughness of spirit must be retained long after the Axis armies are destroyed. It must carry through until every Nazi leader has been brought to justice and every perpetrator of ruthless crimes under Nazi leadership has paid the penalty for violations against God and man.

We in America have never made extravagant claims for democratic government. Under our Constitution the integrity of the American individual is better protected than under any other instrument. We might even say that democratic government has worked miracles during this past year. War production has been miraculous. The striking power of troops, just ordinary men, who until recently were engaged in peace-time pursuits, never wanting to destroy any living thing, has been devastating. People, who love freedom throughout the world, whether in occupied territories or safe in lands where freedom rings, go forward into 1943 confident that the scourge of Adolf Hitler is passing; that the shadow of hatred is receding; that the Nazi pestilence is on the wane. It will seem mysterious and incomprehensible that human beings ever permitted that scourge to gain in strength. Let us hope that now, after ten years of Hitler, we will return to a world where the only mystery will be the love of God "which passeth all understanding."

Our Struggle to Survive

By Rebekah Kohut

In 1932, as I sat in the gardens of Marienbad, I read in the paper that a man named Shickelgruber, who had been holding forth for some time in the beer halls of Munich had stated that the time was coming shortly, when on every signpost and telegraph pole, from Rome to Berlin, there would be the head of a Semite. Figuratively speaking, he has done more than that to the Jewish people. He has destroyed millions of us and many millions he has left physical and spiritual wrecks. And yet, out of the awful slaughter and degradation, there has risen among many of those who are left, a determination to survive, not only as human beings, but as better Jews than the world has known for many years. We shall be able to accomplish this only if among the Jews themselves, there will be a unity of thought and spirit which will be worthy of the great heritage that has been handed down to us by Moses and which we have safeguarded through the centuries, despite the persecution.

Hitler's war is not only against the Jews, it is war that he has laid at the very doorsteps of the Christian people and it is for Christianity to come to its own rescue and thereby the rescue of the Jews. There will always be a division of opinion among groups of people but we can and must, as Jews, respect each other's opinions and endeavor to find their real value. If we do not do so now, we may lose the great opportunity that misery and death have forced upon us; that is, the will to live for the ideals of Judaism.

We as lay people must leave these great decisions to our leaders but as between individuals honesty, justice, integrity, humanity and selflessness are the greatest virtues and ideals, so between nations there must be an end to rivalry and competition and a so-called loyalty and patriotism.

Life has indeed far reaching social implications and its goal is the fashioning of a perfect world in which all of us, Christians and Jews, Reform and Orthodox, must dwell together as equals and mindful of each other's honest opinion. We cannot leave the physical suffering and anguish of our people to the future, but must bring every effort and sacrifice of which we are capable to help them today. We must assert ourselves before all men as crusaders, armed for the struggle to survive, wherever that struggle may drive us. And as for Hitler and his followers, we can leave their fate to the historians and to God. They will receive their just punishment, if indeed enough punishment can be found for them.

The Central Wrong

By Ludwig Lewisohn

It is the mark of our disastrous age that the unimaginable becomes fact. Betrayed by shallow scientific knowledge and the opiate of machinery men forgot that moral differences are the only differences that count. They talked gadgets and business; they were heedless of the command that man is his brother's keeper; they pretended that the abyss had not in 1933 spewed forth primordial evil determined to destroy both the City of man and the City of God.

What happened in that year of doom? Only a few thousands of the best and most upright people in Europe, both Jews and Christians, were being tortured to death for what they *were* and what they represented —the Jewish *ethos* and its inferences in Christianity. So there was apathy and business as usual. For so long as there were gadgets and the multiplication of things, all was considered well in a godless world.

Indifference, pursued by a guilty conscience, *seemed* to deepen; it became actually belligerent in the forms of appeasement in Europe and of isolationism in America. And so those who had had no original share in the historic crime became accessories to it after the fact. Thence sprang the heavy penalty of this long and difficult war—this dark, dark tunnel of deprivation and death through which the United Nations are forced to struggle slowly to the light.

Meanwhile the unspeakable crime continues—the enslavement and humiliation and starvation of Europe, the supreme and symbolic martyrdom of the Jewish people,—that eternal mark of Cain upon the forehead of all mankind! And even yet the peoples of Western Christendom, of the United Nations, have not wholly awakened; even yet none or almost none has come out clearly and spoken out clearly and said: Unless *this* central wrong is righted, unless this symbolic crime is brought to justice, unless this thing that stamps the Anti-Christ *as such* is forevermore remedied, the certain victory of the United Nations will hold a core of moral defeat and of the continuance of evil.

And therefore today, on the tenth anniversary of the beginning of the great crime, when at last we are able to rejoice and do from our hearts rejoice in the beginnings of a military victory for the free men of the West, let us not forget to strive and pray toward the end that this victory remain no mere victory of force but be also a victory of overwhelming right and remember that this cannot be—within the moral world of *all* mankind—unless the symbolic Jewish wrong is righted.

Destiny Confronts America

By Charles H. Tuttle

Until Hitler, political systems of Evil have been careful to tailor themselves in the livery of Good. But Hitler's gospel has been Evil in the raw. In cold blood he has willed the moral and intellectual anarchy of the world in order that amid its ruins there may be none to speak or think or know, except himself. All the lights must go out in order that the Beast can stalk Mankind in darkness.

Through Hitler humanity has learned once for all, but at a ghastly price, that the hate-makers cannot lead into a better world. In the end they enslave not only others but themselves to their own destructive doctrines and conduct. The persecution of one minority leads to the suppression of all minorities. The State which adopts immorality as its ethic must go on and on, unceasingly destroying or bastardizing religion, degrading womanhood, enslaving labor, silencing criticism, and devouring its neighbors.

Unintentionally Hitler has also given the world the greatest and most challenging opportunity in all its history,—the opportunity, born of a common and overwhelming danger and illumined by the fires of a globe-encircling comradeship in arms, to build a New Order upon the eternal foundation that God has made "of one blood all nations of men for to dwell on all the face of the earth".

This is the moment when destiny confronts America with the challenge of Mordecai to Esther "Who knoweth whether thou art come to the kingdom for such a time as this!" The plain people of the world are looking for goals big enough and splendid enough to compensate for all this woe and ruin. Such goals cannot be won by recrudescent nationalism, by economic empire, or by rearrangement of boundaries. They are possible only through a new and militant faith in man as man, a vision of one world indivisible with Liberty and justice for all, the spiritual power needed for the social dynamics of voluntary cooperation, and a universal Bill of Rights for the inalienable freedoms of men, irrespective of race, creed or circumstance.

Righting A Great Wrong
By Henry A. Atkinson

In the ten years since Hitler came into power, he has invaded nearly all the countries of Europe, but has not conquered one of them. Today he faces the greatest crisis in his whole career. The people of the invaded nations have the courage to die rather than to give up their liberty, and thus their will to survive is proving mightier than the strongest weapons Hitler has forged. The Hitler regime has shrouded all Europe in almost total darkness, but we are beginning to see the results of his savagery. Civilization has been set back a thousand years. Hitler's theory of a dominant race based on brutal mass exploitation can hardly be matched in modern or ancient times, and his "wave of the future" is a bloody wave, overwhelming and destroying millions of human beings and all they hold dear. The reprisals against those who try to defend their liberties, the forced labor to keep the Hitler machine rolling, the killing of thousands of hostages mark down Hitler and his coterie of butchers as brutal as any in all history. The underground movements, however, in the occupied countries, including the "satellite" nations—Hungary, Rumania and Italy—indicate that liberty will survive and that there is hope for a new world.

The revelations that have been made recently of the bestial cruelty practiced upon the Jews by order of Hitler and his followers make more clear than anything else the horror and real meaning of Nazi rule. Here we see the deliberate attempt to exterminate all the Jews in Europe. It is conservatively estimated that two million have already been put to death. Jews are condemned without trial and killed without mercy. Millions of Jews have been exiled from their homes and driven out of the countries of which they were citizens. They wander now in Europe without passports or other papers which could establish their status. Persons without a homeland, they can neither legally settle in any country nor pass any frontier because, being stateless, they have no means of securing the necessary permission.

The end of Hitler and his rule is certain. Victory is in sight, but we must not allow false hopes of an early peace to weaken our efforts to continue the battle until a complete armed victory is secure. No adjusted or mediated peace is possible with Hitler, Goering, Goebbels, Himmler, Mussolini, Hirohito, or any others of those who have proved themselves the chief enemies of mankind.

The churches and church people of the world have resting upon them a great responsibility, for it is only in so-called Christian lands that anti-Semitism flourishes in its most dangerous form. The church should take this to heart seriously and join with the United Nations in their demand that the slaughter of innocent Jews be stopped and stopped immediately, and that those who are actually carrying out the executions be punished for this crime.

The number of Jews still in imminent danger in Europe will reach three or four millions, possibly more. Some way to rescue them should be found, and this rescue work should be carried out at once. It seems that the only immediate solution is for the United Nations to support Great Britain and the United States in an appeal for opening wide the doors of Palestine to immigration, and at the same time make plans whereby through some kind of quota system each nation, including our own, can at once take its share of refugees.

What the Jews have lost should be made a specific and first charge against the reparation and repatriation funds. The right of the Jews to return to their former homes should be in the Peace Treaty, and those who prefer should be allowed to settle in Palestine and become citizens of the Jewish state. But a most important way to help settle this question will be for the United Nations to recognize that even the appearance of political anti-Semitism is an incitement to aggression and, as such, should be made punishable under international law.

Just as Hitler has made his attack on the Jews the basis of his campaign against the liberties of all free men everywhere, so the United Nations should use the establishment of security for the Jewish victims of Hitler's hate the basis of their approach for righting a great wrong and laying the foundations of freedom from fear and freedom from want for all the peoples in all lands.

Liberty—For All People

By W. Warren Barbour
United States Senator from New Jersey

AMONG the many post war problems with which the United Nations will be confronted, one of the most complex admittedly will be the problem of the uprooted, disinherited, and all but decimated European Jewry.

The civilized world now accepts the fact that no man has the right to enslave the mind and body of another. Century after century, the Jew might have compromised his faith and even appeased his oppressors —but by so doing—he would have forsaken the watchword of democracy—liberty. Freedom and liberty are the inalienable rights of all mankind and it is for these great principles that we are now engaged in this worldwide conflict—because they mean FREEDOM.

Wherever tyranny threatens, wherever the rights of man and the four freedoms are in danger of being destroyed, there you will find the Jew joining forces with others willing to fight and die for freedom. That is one of the reasons Hitler took special pains to single out the Jews for persecution and, if possible, complete annihilation.

None of us must fail to realize the tremendous importance of the next twelve months. We know that the duration and course of this war possibly will be decided within that time. The decision may be forged in the sea lanes of the South Pacific, or on the sands of North Africa, or even on the continent of Europe itself. The decision will rest largely upon the speed with which we here in America turn out the necessary equipment and sinews of war. We at home are privileged to have but a small part, but one of the principal parts in the decision of the battle to come will be played right here at home by the great cross-section of the masses of the American people. If our people shirk their duty or allow themselves to be *disunited*, that battle will be decided against us. But I have great faith in America, great faith in her people—all her people—regardless of race, creed, or color. But just as surely as we are united—self-sacrificing, brave, we must also be tolerant and understanding, both in mind and spirit.

America has a great tradition of freedom—much of that tradition comes from the Old Testament. The crossing of the Atlantic Ocean to reach the promised land of America by our first settlers has its parallel in the crossing of the Red Sea by those Jews in flight to a new freedom. When America fought for independence, the story of God destroying the yoke of Egypt gave spiritual justification for our expression of the right of all men to liberty. In this new struggle for liberty we find Jews rendering service of the highest quality, being among the first to give their lives for the country whose abiding democratic principles stem from the tenets of their own religious history.

This is not a war on the part of America merely to avenge Pearl Harbor. Those who hate the people who make up America hate our country and all it stands for. To us in this country, it is a call to preserve once and for all time our free way of life—to preserve once and for all, for all people—LIBERTY.

Bloody Anniversary

By Fannie Hurst

It is ten terrible years, bloody anniversary, since the cloud which has always been bigger than a man's hand, began to spread its threat over the face of the earth.

That hand, growing to its horrible maturity, has strangled human happiness in a manner that is probably unprecedented, even in the history of a human race which has shed blood and tears for so many centuries.

Unfortunately, it is not the hand of Herr Hitler. It is not that simple. That hand, even at its evil best, is mortal and fallible. Its span of life cannot greatly exceed three-score-and-ten. To be sure, it is a foul, a defiled and defiling hand. It is smeared with blood, it is wetted with tears, it is corroded with the leprosy of evil.

And yet behind him lurks a hand even more menacing than the one which motivates the evil that this man doeth. Forces larger than he is, even more potently evil than he is, have made him possible.

That the world's billions of people should have allowed him to destroy, ravage, rape and degrade the human race, brings us up sharply and bitterly to the conclusion that it is not alone the hand of Hitler that must be vanquished.

Plans are already afoot to bring those bloody-handed men who have been leaders in cruelty, intolerance and meting out human anguish for the past decade, before a post-war court of justice. That is as it should be. But that is not enough.

Those billions of men and women who have not hated hate sufficiently; whose intolerance of intolerance has either been non-existent or supine, must also be brought before tribunal.

What is society prepared to do about itself following this war? Before what tribunal will it answer? What plans are in the making for the post-war handling of this root of the evil? Day of reckoning for Hitler and Mussolini, Hirohito and their tribe, is not enough. Even while these murderers are facing their tribunal, millions of children are being educated to carry on their hateful way of life.

Deeply incorporated into the pattern of a post-war world fit to live in, must be an educational scheme, policed if necessary, which will inculcate in the generations to come, qualities which will not tolerate the kind of world which made Hitler possible.

Human race, look inward!

Beyond Human Belief

By *Alfred E. Smith*

OF course I am more than glad to join with you and your associates in the sad commemoration of ten years of Hitlerism in your forthcoming issue devoted to that subject.

The impact of Hitler's campaign for the mass destruction of the Jews leaves me and many of our countrymen stunned by a series of horrors which are so far beyond human belief that we could not credit them to any less vicious a group than the Nazis.

We are fighting a war against these people for many reasons but surely one of the greatest of these reasons is the hope that through a complete victory over these loathsome beings we can eradicate the shadow of death and slavery from the lives of what poor remnant may remain of the Jewish population of Eastern Europe. Such a thought will, I know, give every American added incentive for the quick winning of this war.

It is an honor to join with you and your colleagues to do what we can to bring this about.

Hitlerism — A Meditation

By Bishop Ralph Spaulding Cushman

ONE cannot review the frightful and foul story of Nazi arrogance and cruelty without recognizing that this hideous movement is directly and indirectly an attack upon essential religion. Whatever one thinks of Hitler's grandiose declarations that he would tear up Christianity and Judaism root and branch, or of the brutal murders and inhuman treatment of subject peoples—especially the Jews—it all amounts to the same thing, an attack upon religion.

Bismarck once said that the nation that gives up God is like the nation that gives up territory. But Hitler and his followers will learn that there is more ʌvolved than territory. Human welfare is at stake in this matter of religion. Reverence for the Father-God and compassion for humanity eternally go together. In recent weeks Hitler has begun to talk about "God"—but his talk has not as yet checked the massacres of Polish people. It is significant that the same prophet who said "What doth the Lord require of thee but to do justly, to love mercy, and to walk humbly with thy God", was also the prophet who prophesied concerning the day when nations "shall beat their swords into ploughshares and their spears into pruninghooks: nation shall not lift up the sword against nation".

Perhaps it is a rediscovery of the fact of the vital

relationship between the sincere worship of God and a merciful regard for humanity that is causing the talk in secular quarters at the present time about a "revival" of religion, "nothing but religion can help the world out of the mess we are in".

But in the eyes of God "humanity" is inclusive. God is no respecter of persons,—not even in America. Perhaps the super-sin of Hitlerism is this super-race sin; this attempt to build a super-religion upon the selfish and devilish premise that the Germans are a super-race.

One of the things that this scourge of war (let us pray) may do for the average man—without or within the Church—is to bring to him the rediscovery of the fact that reverence for God and concern for human welfare are forever inseparable.

After all it is futile to review the horrors of Hitlerism unless we ourselves are going to learn some lessons that may lead us to repent of our own sins. Supernationalism can never build the new world for which we pray. It would seem that "isolationism" is passing out in America in these days of global war. May we cherish the new light when the war is at an end.

It Must Not Be In Vain

By Alonzo F. Myers

THE persecution, the suffering, the bloodshed, and the destruction produced by ten years of Hitlerism must not have been in vain. We must all look back with deepest regret and chagrin upon our failure to have acted promptly in preventing Hitler's march of destruction. We can all look forward with hope and courage to the day, not too far distant, when Hitler and his followers will be destroyed .

Let us resolve now that we shall never again be complacent in the face of persecution and exploitation of our fellow men. The blessings of democracy, justice, and equality must be extended to the people of all nations, regardless of their color, creed, or economic status. That is the crusade in which men of good faith through all the world must be enlisted now while the horrors of Hitlerism are fresh in their minds. Only so can we prevent the inevitable tendency to relax when the specific enemy has been defeated. Only so can we prevent future wars and future sufferings and persecution.

Without Mercy

By Thomas Mann

Time and again I have expressed my profound horror of the atrocious deeds of the Nazi regime, and I shall certainly not miss this opportunity to do it again. Among the idiotic crimes which these fiends commit all over Europe the mass extermination of the Jews stands out as particularly frightful.

Just recently I have had news that the eighty-six year old widow of the great painter Max Liebermann has been deported to Poland without mercy, despite serious efforts by the Swedish Embassy in Berlin. This is one individual case only, but one which particularly outrages me as an artist and friend of the late master and his house.

Never has a nation been more degraded by its rulers than the German nation. The military defeat that it will suffer will not humiliate it half as much as it has been humiliated for ten years by those men into whose ruthless hands it has fallen. On the contrary, we must hope that the catastrophe which it will meet, will be the beginning of its resurrection.

The Darkest Decade

By John Haynes Holmes

I wonder if there is any decade in history so black as the ten years of Adolf Hitler. It paralyzes thought, to say nothing of emotion, to contemplate the sum total of human misery, despair and death packed into this period of the dominance of one man over the world of human affairs. This sum total, of course, we do not know, as history will never know, for there is a point where a swirling flood passes the bounds of measurement. But we know enough to know that so many people have never suffered so much in so short a period of time.

Retribution must be terrible. It has already begun in the case of the German people dragged slowly down to a doom of destruction greater than anything that they have endured since the Thirty Years' War. It will continue in the plunge of Hitler himself into the depths of horror now yawning for him. But we shall err if we seek vengeance upon this man, or find satisfaction in that vengeance of inexorable fate which is the divine vengeance of which Paul spoke. Our task if not so much to condemn Hitler as a monster as to understand him as an historical phenomenon. How happens it that such a creature as he could master a nation, enslave a continent, dominate an age, and throw a whole world into the throes of suicidal war? How did this man ever emerge, much less rise to power? There's a question for us! And it points right straight to something wrong with us and our world as well as with him and his gang. The Nazis qualify as dragon's teeth. How do we qualify as sowers of these teeth?

Lift the Yoke of Oppression

By Herbert H. Lehman
Director, Foreign Relief and Rehabilitation Operations

I understand that OPINION is about to publish a special issue entitled, "Ten Years of Hitler." Incredibly, year by year Hitler's bestiality has continued to grow until now it has reached such a crescendo of horror that it is inconceivable his followers do not recognize him for the madman he is. Only in the mind of a maniac could Hitler's latest terrible atrocity be hatched. Never before in the history of the world has any tyrant plotted the mass extermination of a whole people. Such an overwhelming horror has stunned all civilized people. It is beyond understanding that human beings can participate in such sickening, loathsome savagery.

Our fight for justice and liberty can only end in triumph and the Nazi menace must be wiped from the face of the earth forever. I hope and pray that peace may come soon. But we can afford no halfway victory. We must win the peace as well as the war. We and the rest of the United Nations must gird ourselves to make every sacrifice for the total annihilation of the Nazi monsters who are devoid of all sense of human decency. Those brutal, ruthless forces of Nazidom must not be allowed ever again the remotest chance to spread and practice their evil doctrines.

We face this New Year of 1943 with a brighter outlook, but this does not mean that we can relax in the slightest degree our determination to stamp out for all time the curse fostered on the entire world by Hitler and his satellites.

I pray with all my heart that the yoke of oppression and suffering soon will be lifted from our pitiful, unfortunate co-religionists abroad.

Our Cause Will Triumph

By George Gordon Battle
Co-Chairman, Council Against Intolerance in America

Due to the evil influence of Hitlerism, the past decade has been without doubt the most disastrous and the most tragic era in the history of the world. We have had military conquerors, actuated by personal ambition, such as Alexander and Napoleon, whose armies have cause widespread desolation. We have had barbaric leaders, such as Attila, who have ravaged the land over which they passed. But never have we had such a figure as Hitler, who proclaims with brazen boastfulness that he despises and utterly disregards all the fundamental laws of truth and justice and humanity, who announces that he is relying upon the policy of deceit, of falsehood, of bigotry, and of brutal cruelty, in order to attain universal domination. And furthermore he and his adherents follow this inhuman course of conduct not through ignorance but with the avowed purpose of trampling upon all the restrictions and rules of humanity and of religion. They are the open enemies of all that is good, of all that is spiritual. He and his allies, by striking suddenly and treacherously at an unprepared world, have attained during the past ten years an amazing degree of success. But at the beginning of this second era we are glad and happy to note that every evil assault has been checked; that the strength of righteousness is beginning to overwhelm these forces of evil. In Europe, in Asia, and throughout the Seven Seas, the German and the Japanese governments, united by a common policy of treachery and cruelty (together with the puppet government of Mussolini) are meeting reverses everywhere. Their advance has been halted. They are now on the defensive. As we here in this Western hemisphere bring into play our great powers of organization and of production, our armies on land, on sea and in air will grow strong and stronger. The cause of the angels must and will eventually triumph. We are sure that under a just God victory will eventually and we hope before many months be ours.

Perhaps the most disgusting and most dangerous phase of the Hitler regime has been its appeal to religious and racial intolerance and bigotry. Nothing like it has been seen in the annals of mankind—not even in the Dark Ages. All right thinking men and women everywhere will rejoice that the axe has already been laid at the root of this evil growth. It is at this vital spot that the Enemy has aimed his strongest attack. It is failing. It will collapse. And in God's good time his cause of righteousness will triumph.

Civilization is Aroused

By Jeremiah T. Mahoney

THE year 1943 marks the tenth year of Hitlerism or the tenth anniversary of Germanic degradation, decline, barbarous persecution, and man's inhumanity to man. When the innumerable crimes committed in the name of Nazism are finally recorded and this appalling carnage and devastation is followed by a complete and total victory for the courageous and the just, our children will have the right to ask why this monster was ever permitted to build himself and his frightful system into an engine of destruction, able to encompass so many peoples and to subjugate so much of the world.

The young people of the world will have the right to criticize those statesmen of the world, including our own, who failed or refused to foresee the consequences of the Hitler menace as it grew, and to crush it before it vented its spleen upon a peaceful world.

It was evident to many, who spoke out at the birth of Hitlerism, that the initial Nazi discrimination against the German Jew was but a cloak for enlarged ambition to enslave all who opposed the Nazi ideology, and who refused to become chattels of an unmoral political movement. In *Mein Kampf*, Hitler himself sounded a warning to the world of his ambitions were he placed in a position to act. Yet the majority of the statesmen of the world, whose duty it was to speak.

remained silent and permitted Hitler and his minions to continue their ruthless program unopposed.

The resolutions of the Nazi Party at conferences held in Nuremberg and elsewhere should have been proof sufficient to the world that this daring adventurer felt that he could conquer the world, and by creating fear among all peoples, accomplish his vicious plan with little or no opposition. Except for ignoble and selfish reasons, England and France could have stopped Hitler almost before he started, and in spite of the procrastination of these nations, effective action nevertheless could have been compelled, if the leading statesmen of the rest of the world had taken a proper stand and utilized decent world opinion.

Some brave individuals and courageous organizations did protest. Many dedicated to the service of God raised their voices against the vile persecution of Jew and Christian alike. These became the first public victims of Nazi fury and hate, while thousands less prominent and known only to God, lie in unmarked graves, the silent and hushed evidence of Nazi brutality.

Now, thank God, civilization long asleep, is aroused. It has come forth from the depths of lethargy and is on the high road to victory and an enlightened peace. The united nations face the future with determination that what has happened under Hitler shall never occur again. The chicanery of statesmen or the selfish interests of nations must never again be allowed to endanger the peace of struggling humanity. We pray God for total victory, and with trust and confidence in Him, civilization shall survive and once again reflect His glory.

Challenge to the World

By A. Philip Randolph
President, Brotherhood of Sleeping Car Porters

THE wanton murder, indescribable persecution and cruel terrorism of the Jewish people in Europe by the wicked Nazi agents of Hitler, shocks the conscience of every normal, decent, civilized human being.

The barbarian hordes of Attila are mild ministers of mercy to these ruthless forces of evil, death and destruction under this mad man of Germany.

This attack and expressed will to annihilate the Jewish people, is an attack upon the whole civilized world—Negroes, Christians, trade unionists, Americans, women and children.

It is a challenge not only to defeat and execute Hitler and his co-conspirators, but also to wipe out Hitlerism, root and branch, in Germany, Europe, Great Britain, and the entire world, including our own United States of America.

Obliterate the Evil

By William Allen White

Hitler's ten years proves what a terrible thing can be done when one man with maniacal unrestraint and a talent for magnificent falsehood and unchecked cruelty can incarnate in his leadership all the evil in men's hearts which rises out of the injustices that are caused by man's inhumanity to man. If there is any such definite force as evil operating in this world, it functioned from 1933 to 1943 in the leadership of Adolph Hitler. It was almost as though the Biblical devil, Milton's Lucifer, who fought with God, had come back to earth again.

I know of no other period in modern history when all the wickedness that clusters around hate was so perfectly organized with the skill of modern technology as it has been brought together to serve the Hitler regime. Hate, which is of course a physical lust of the heart, has become under Hitler almost a spiritual force of evil in the body and mind of one man.

But he alone is not to blame. Indeed it is too late now to assess the blame. And it is not too late to crush, obliterate and remove from this earth not merely the evil that men have done in Hitler's name, but also to wipe out of western civilization the crass and heartbreaking injustices that assembled the evil and gave Hitler power.

Victory to Safeguard the Future

By Herbert Bayard Swope

H ITLER has not merely fought Mankind. He has assailed that life which we have struggled to gain, to hold and to better since the Dark Ages. He has set the clock back untold years. It will be, at least, a generation before that clock can be rewound; and a longer time before it is running properly.

If those who take up the sword shall die by the sword, then the Nazis and the Japs have shown us an easy way of firmly establishing victory — by the favored road of liquidation. But we shall not do that, although the logic of war would justify it. The Nazis and their allies have demonstrated the impossibility of a world existing half-Nazi and half-free; but, instead of wiping out their evil roots by force, we shall have to begin on a process of education—compulsory at first; then, it is to be hoped, freely chosen by those who see the light.

First, we must win. We must win effectively and finally. We must achieve not a doodad of a victory, but one that is forthright and complete—so complete as to permit the will of an enlightened world to be imposed upon those who have defied humanity. We shall not permit ourselves to be stopped either by the machinations of the traitors and the appeasers or the false sentimentalists and irresponsible pacifists.

The Nazis have tried to reduce the stature of Man. We must render them forever incapable of attempting this experiment again.

Design for Murder

By *Alvin Johnson*

TEN years of Hitler: ten years of deliberately planned, systematic murder.

Murder has always been an incident to usurpation, to conquest. But hitherto, in the Western world, attempts have been made to cover it up, to explain it away. It remained for Hitler to make of murder the central constructive item in his design. History will rank Hitler as an inventor in the field of politics, inventor of a political machine driven and sustained by crime.

Possibly at the outset Hitler himself was unawakened to the political dynamics of murder. Possibly he felt something of a shock when his poisonous drivellings produced their first murder. But with the instinct of an inventor he perceived that the men who participated in the first mob killing were bound together by a stronger force than devotion to a leader, gratitude for favors to come. They were bound together by the cohesive force of complicity in crime.

More mobs, more murders: an ever extending circle of followers held together by complicity in crime. To get a whole people within the circle: this would be Hitler's triumph. Perhaps it might not be possible to draw the plain German, traditionally humane, immediately into the circle of murder, but he could be drawn into complicity in the crime of spoliation. He could be induced to stone the windows of a Jewish

57

home, to yell insults, to spit in the face of a terrified Jew. But the descent to approving concentration camps and the nameless horrors committed there was swift. Hitler's invention was working. Virtually the whole people had been forged into a unity by complicity in crime.

"They are making us universally hated," an old peasant complained in 1934. Exactly that was Hitler's need. It gave him a universal cause of war against the world that hated Hitlerite Germany. He could count on his criminal following—a whole people —to invade and crush and enslave, for was not all the world enemy? The democratic peoples might indeed forget and forgive pecadilloes like the seizure of Austria, the destruction of Czechoslovakia. They forgot and forgave the Armenian massacres. There lay the danger for Hitler's plan. The German people might return to a civilized mood, if the world seemed capable of treating bygones as bygones. Recall the rage of Hitler when Chamberlain appeared at Munich with his umbrella of forgiveness. More crime, more crime, was the need of Hitler's machine. Invade, rob, rape, murder—not, as puzzled civilized men suppose, to employ the outmoded technique of terrorism—for the first World War proved that terrorism does not work. No: to stir up the universal hatred of mankind, in order to cement the unity of the German people.

And now, when the military power of the United Nations is developing toward ascendancy, and the Germans are losing the victory morale—the only morale they have lived by in the past—what can the inventor

Hitler do? At all costs he must build up the morale of complicity in crime, colossal, unforgivable crime. It is this that explains the murder of hostages, the wiping out of villages, the ghastly killing of hundreds of thousands of Jews in Poland, men old and young, women, little children, all helpless and harmless. Does he do it in secret? All the world knows of it. Hitler wants the world to know of it, that the German people may count on condign punishment if they yield.

The Germans would be contemplating a negotiated peace today, if they could have peace without punishment. But they know that the wrath of the peoples is strong against them. Better die fighting, like criminals cornered.

This is the morale on which Hitler the inventor is building. Sooner or later, however, the German people will realize how they have been beguiled into crime to serve Hitler's criminal purposes, how the German name has been disgraced for all time. Hitler and his henchmen will cry out to the victors for protection against their maddened people.

The wrath of God, slow but terrible, is gathering.

The Limits of Indecency
By Irwin Edman

I FEEL very much as if I were partaking in a kind of black mass, a Devil's worship or a general hellish hulla-baloo participating in a "celebration" of Ten Years of Hitler. What on earth or in air can one find new to say on this subject? Perhaps one thing one can find is that one should not allow the horror to come to seem stale and old and routine. In the old optimistic liberal days of my own college generation I thought it would never again be possible to speak in terms of a battle between good and evil. I remember smiling, even as a high school boy, at Theodore Roosevelt when he announced that he stood at Armageddon and battled for the Lord. I could not help wondering where he got the appointment or the license. Even then I presumed it was poetic license.

Nor am I even now by way of thinking that all good is on the side of the Allied Nations. We obviously have our own houses to clean and we are far from realizing democracy in industry, politics or education. There are sinister and Fascist forces at work among us too, but the fact remains that we are, all things considered, a million light years ahead of the intention of the Axis powers, particularly, I suspect, Germany.

The lesson for a moralist of the past ten years seems to me so patent that it is by way of becoming banal. One simply cannot avoid the danger of political evil becoming epidemic in the world. The war, if it has done nothing else so far, has made it perfectly clear that there come certain limits in the violation of human decency which cannot be allowed to go on because the world itself cannot go on in a civilized way if these evils continue.

I do not know that there is anything further I can add. A re-recital of the horrors of Hitlerism, a re-fortifying of our own convictions that they must be extirpated; all this has been done over and over again and by better hands. That these things are true almost goes without saying. But for almost ten years they went without very much being done about them. The point of the whole conflict is that at long last something at great but recognized cost is being done about it.

Reminder to Free Peoples

By Robert J. Watt
International Representative, American Federation of Labor

ALTHOUGH free peoples all over the world are suffering under the assault of Hitler and his hate-poisoned Nazis, the plight of the Jewish people who are bravely resisting slavery in all the enslaved nations is tragic beyond words.

Their plight must serve as a reminder to all free peoples what is in store for them unless we fully recognize that we face an avowed foe who has no scruples as to the viciousness or intensity of his effort or its consequences to mankind.

Their plight must serve as a reminder to all free peoples that we are faced by the actual fact that the Nazi gangsters who now enslave almost all of continental Europe have undertaken to force out of existence any system of government, religion, economics or society which does not goosestep at their command.

Those of us who are not of the Jewish faith must be reminded again and again that although Jews were the first to be oppressed by the Nazi brutes, the followers of other religions have also felt the cruel heel whenever and wherever the Nazis have bludgeoned control.

We must be reminded that free peoples cannot continue to make their lives and jobs secure and improve their standards of living while at the same time everything that is decent is being shattered in other parts of the world by the Nazi plunderbund.

And lest we forget we must be reminded again that civilization has long owed a debt of gratitude to the Jewish people for the magnificent contribution they have made to the building of the foundations of the institution of government and to the responsibilities of the individual to the community.

The hideous suffering of Jewish men, women and children has not dulled their courage to resist slavery. They have demonstrated that they love liberty and homeland more than they feel torture or fear death. Tomorrow their greatness will live again undaunted by the foul swastika.

May we, while we march in the same ranks against the same foes, be given the strength to establish the same pattern of courage, so that our great melting pot may become the foundry from which mankind may fuse again the institutions of liberty and democracy and brotherhood among the people of the world.

The Task Ahead

By Max Lerner

At the end of a decade of Hitlerism there are now at least a substantial nucleus of men and women all over the world who understand its true character. Most of them have had to learn slowly and have paid in blood and agony for the slowness of their learning.

The war is not yet won, either in the world or within America itself. There will be further outcroppings of Hitlerism to be dealt with even after the war. But one thing we can say: these movements of native Fascism will no longer be aided, as they were during the past decade, by the prestige of Nazi power. That power, and the might of Nazi invincibility have now been destroyed.

The mark of their destruction is seen in the blood and fire of the Russian offensives. It is seen in the huddled remnants of Rommel's army, scattered in flight across North Africa. It is seen in the shattered diplomatic prestige of Germany, and in the dissension among the Nazi generals. It is seen in Hitler's own aging, pouchy, paranoid face. It is seen in the pathos of the lives of the German common people, who must now bear not only the agony of Nazi exploitation but also the agony of a losing war. It is seen in the increasing terrorism to which the Nazis have had to resort against the Jews and the other peoples of Europe: for a ruling group that cannot rule by strength must rule by violence and terror, and rulers who are panicky before defeat are the rulers who go berserk and who will seek to bring the world down to destruction along with themselves.

There remains for us to finish the war, not as a war of survival but as a war for a free world and a democratic world order. There remains for us to unify the progressive forces of every religious persuasion and every nation-state for the task that lies ahead. That task will be as difficult in the decade to come as it has been in the decade past: but the stakes this time are not just survival, but a world fit for the effort of freedom and the adventure of democracy.

The Last Laugh

By Frank Kingdon

T HERE is laughter in Europe.

It is the laughter of men who line victims against a wall and laugh to see them shot.

It is the laughter of men who whisper the obscenities of sadism behind closed doors.

It is the laughter of men who are mad with diabolical illusions of superiority and power.

It is the laughter of men who are drunk on the red wine of hate and death.

It is the laughter of men who have damned civilization as a lie and who have condemned morality as a falsehood.

They laugh—these men—standing in a pool of blood heavy with cruel suffering as though the Four Horsemen had spilled it riding ruthless over field and home.

There are tears in Europe.

They are the tears of women torn from all they love.

They are the tears of children who have seen their fathers die.

They are the hot bitter tears of men who have seen their women beaten before their helpless eyes.

They are the tears of the dreamers and the makers who have seen Beauty crushed by men in whom the spirit has died.

They are the tears of the godly who have seen their altars spat upon and their scrolls trampled underfoot.

They weep—these sufferers—but their weeping is no weakness, rather is it the purging of their hearts and the watering of their springs of hope and faith from which their strength is nourished.

And their strength is greater than the power of the men who laugh now.

This is a moral universe.

Justice will not fulfill itself in our universe until every last drop of innocent blood spilled has been repaid from the veins of those whose evil can know no atonement at any lesser price.

There is another laughter. It comes from far places. It is terrible in the ears of all who arrogate false pride to themselves.

It is the last laugh.

"The kings of the earth set themselves, and the rulers take counsel together against the Lord and against his people."

But

"He that sitteth in the heavens shall laugh; the Lord shall have them in derision."

God's laughter is Hitler's judgment.

He shall not escape it.

Climax of Iniquity

By *William H. Kilpatrick*

Words fail as one attempts to describe and denounce Hitlerism. Mine at least are inadequate.

In general—to speak calmly even if one does not so feel—Hitlerism is in its ethics and social outlook the denial and negation of the essence of civilized life as this is judged by the historic consensus of the world's moral leaders.

In particular, to single out the Jew—as Hitler has done—for the most cruel and unjust persecution in human history adds to positive social immorality the further evil of diseased thinking. Of it all, the latest horror of mass extermination stands as the climax of iniquity. Even to write it down in words fills one with utter loathing.

The whole decent world owes it to civilization—yea, to its own moral self-respect—to right these wrongs, to wipe out the curse of Hitlerism along with the entire Axis effort. To this end we fight and shall fight to the full conclusion.

Rebuilding Civilization

By Mary Anderson
Director, Women's Bureau United States Department of Labor

In the past ten years of intensive struggle by the Jewish race under Hitlerism, OPINION should be congratulated on holding aloft the torch of hope and inspiration for those who have suffered so greatly.

I think two groups of human beings in particular have been persecuted by the Nazi regime, the Jewish people and women. The regimentation of the human mind and spirit as well as of the body, the cruelties perpetrated on suffering humanity, and the flood of violence and death let loose on the world by Hitler and his followers, have put a blot on the history of mankind that can never be erased unless we build a much better world with security and freedom for all people, regardless of creed, race or color, regardless of whether they are men or women.

All my life I have striven especially for improved standards and policies concerning the welfare of wage-earning women, for I have always agreed with those who say that the status of women in any community is an index of the degree of its civilization. We have only to look at the way the position of women in Germany has fallen in the past ten years to see how civilization there has declined. The happy home life of Germans in the early part of the twentieth century is gone. Fathers and mothers now are spied upon by children who belong to the Nazi state, and whose only god is a gangster on an international scale. Women in Germany, no matter what blood runs in their veins, have been reduced to serfdom under Hitlerism.

Merely to wipe out the Nazis and the organization responsible for all this, will require a supreme effort on the part of each one of us in the United Nations, working together in close cooperation. But after we have learned to do this successfully, to wipe out Hitlerism will not be enough. We must go on working together in the more difficult, more complex task of building a better world which will provide for all growing children, as well as for all men and for all women, freedom from war, terror and want, freedom to work and play and live together in peace and happiness.

Global war has forced us to think in world terms. Have we learned this lesson thoroughly enough to continue to think and act in global terms? Are we willing to pay the price of peace, to make the sacrifices which peaceful relations between nations will demand? The building of a better world will take many years, for it will come only as a result of the patient, joint effort of all who have suffered, of all who have been persecuted, whether in greater or less degree. And as industrial studies have shown that women often do well those jobs which require patience, so I trust that women everywhere will prove adept at the cooperation essential to rebuilding a civilization better than the one which has gone down after ten years of attack by Hitler and like-minded men.

This Black Decade

By Solomon Goldman

I T IS too late at the end of this black decade, indeed it
would be nothing short of blasphemous in the face of
the ruin it has wrought, to seek relief in calling Hitler
names or in denouncing Hitlerism. "I beheld the earth,
and lo, it was waste and void; and the heavens, and they
had no light. I beheld the mountains and lo, they
trembled, and all the hills moved to and fro. I beheld,
and lo, there was no man, and all the birds of the
heavens were fled. I beheld, and lo, the fruitful field was
a wilderness, and all the cities thereof were broken
down."

Every school boy now knows that Hitlerism is the
enemy of freedom and dignity and, consequently, of
civilization and religion. It is the successful reversion
to primitivism. It is man in the raw. It is the jungle,
swallowing up again the clearing which men have made
in it. That is today common knowledge.

It is sad and tragic that it took a thousand con-
flagrations before we recognize the hellish fire, and ten
thousand holocausts before we smelled its foul odor.
Why the world needed such a prolonged nightmare
before it identified the Frankenstein, the Jew alone
knows, and every issue of OPINION during this decade
testifies to it. Hitlerism had the immunity of anti-Semitism. Hitler's insanity, his plans against Western civili-

zation, were veiled from the world by its complacency to his persecution of the Jews. He was neither ingenious nor original. He only bettered the example of a long line of "honorable," "civilized" European gentlemen. He took all the maledictions of bigotry, all the innuendoes of misgovernment, all the accusations of incompetence, and smelted them into one molten mass. Many centuries of insane Jew-baiting made their contribution to the amalgam. It was, for a time, good doctrine that we were the devil's community, referred to in the Apocalypse, and our only preoccupation was the desecration of the Name. Men were taught that. "They do not have to be concerned about this people, destined for destruction . . . to show them kindliness or give them shelter is a sin."

Here is why two million Jews were sadistically put to death, and why Europe was, at the same time, laid waste. OPINION has told this story more than once.

But even as it is too late to berate Hitler, it is far more insufferable, loathsome and humiliating to beg for mercy, to speak of defense, to argue with the anti-Semite or to play at the game of good will. It is too late, too late. There is no balm in the friendly words of a conclave of Bishops or in the mournful resolutions of parliaments, or in the sympathetic messages of Presidents and Prime Ministers.

Anti-Semitism has ceased to be a Jewish problem. It is a Christian disease. It is no longer a Jewish woe but the world's misfortune. It must be eradicated by means of a stupendous effort, even as Hitler, root, trunk and branch. It must be destroyed in our metropolitan newspapers that advertise "Gentiles only," in our great universities — pity their greatness — that

whisper *numerus clausus*, in our large industries that
lie, lie and lie.

Anti-Semitism perished in godless Russia. Who and
what keeps it alive in Christian lands? If this last
decade has not cured the world of anti-Semitism, then
fie on civilization.

Reconstruction and Rehabilitation

By Henry Smith Leiper

As year has followed tragic year the unspeakable horror and brutality of Hitlerism has increased rather than diminished. No decade in history, has been more truly a decade of infamy. And at long last people everywhere know what they should long ago have known —that his defeat concerns absolutely every decent man and woman in the world.

Upon no single group has so heavy a share of suffering fallen as upon the Jewish people; and the hearts of all Christians who have any right to the name are touched with sadness and sympathy. Would that Christians everywhere had been willing to listen when some of us told them in 1933 what the program of Hitler would mean not only for the Jew but for all mankind!

There is a kind of retribution which falls upon those who ask "Am I my brother's keeper?"—and it has fallen upon many blind Christians who took no thought concerning the fate of the Jew when he alone seemed to be the object of Hitlerian terrorism and plundering. One cannot rejoice at such retribution; but there is something of justice in it which wise men will see.

As we win a military victory over Hitler and all his hoard of thugs and criminals—and win we shall—there will come a time of reconstruction and rehabilitation. In that day, soon to dawn we trust, may there be a new kind of cooperation between all those who bow the knee to the God of Abraham, Isaac and Jacob! It will be needed if there is to be built a new order insured against the recurrence of world catastrophe. Despite all their differences Jew and Christian alike possess the basic faith needed for such a task of reordering human relations.

It is an impressive fact that the five things in the realm of faith most hated by Hitler are the things which all heirs of the Bible tradition have in common: faith in God as man's creator and judge; faith in man as a potential son of God—with certain inalienable rights flowing from that paternity; faith in universal human brotherhood in the one family of the One God; faith in the moral law as representing the immutable and universal will of the Creator; and faith in the possibility of man's redemption from selfishness and sin through the freely offered pardon and renewal of a loving Heavenly Father.

May we who share that fivefold faith learn to live it together as we face tomorrow's world! Only by so doing shall we earn the right to a lasting peace.

The Most Monstrous Evil

By Frank E. Gannett

To celebrate "ten years of Hitler" is to mark an infamous anniversary. It can only result in good if it helps to bring home to the American people—and to all others throughout the world who, with them, love liberty and hate oppression—the magnitude and the threat of the forces marshalled and led by the leader of German Nazism.

To enumerate the crimes of Hitler is to repeat a catalog of sins utterly abhorrent. Everything which we hold precious, worth living and fighting for, finds its opposite and its mortal enemy in the philosophy and the political tenets of Adolph Hitler. As a consequence, it has been difficult—and too often impossible—for Americans to believe many of the completely authenticated instances of Nazi barbarities.

Beginning with thousands of the German people themselves, and spreading throughout the continent as Nazi conquests grew, such hardships, oppressions and crimes have been visited upon the millions of occupied Europe as cannot be matched unless one goes back to the ancient world or to the Tartar invasions. Especially has the Nazi's treatment of the Jew been of such a character as to defy any possibility of adequate description.

It is well to remind ourselves of these facts as we face the tenth anniversary of Hitler's rise to power in Germany, the beginning of the whole series of horrible events which have intervened. Only as we realize that these things are facts, and not the product of fearful shock and resentment, can we grasp the threat which Nazism is to us and to all we hold dear.

Let us make this anniversary an occasion to renew our adherence to everything we most deeply cherish; to all those things guaranteed us by our own Bill of Rights; to all those impulses toward goodwill and brotherhood, toward mutual understanding and common effort, which find their roots and inspiration in the Judeo-Christian religious heritage.

For us and our brothers across the seas there can be no thought of differences of religion, race, creed or political conviction. For us there is neither bond nor free, neither Gentile nor Jew, neither foreigner nor native son. There must be only unity of purpose against the most monstrous evil which has ever assailed human freedom and rights.

Necessary Lessons

By Robert E. Speer

THESE "Ten years of Hitler" should reteach us lessons which all history has been teaching but which we have never learned:

1. That for good or ill mankind is one body, all races of one blood, and that it must live a common life, that if one member suffers, all members will suffer with it.

2. That the common life of mankind requires instrumentalities by which it may function:—in political terms, a body of common law, a court to apply this law, and an authority to enforce it.

3. That it does matter what men think—that the falsehoods of "Mein Kampf" are not mere harmless personal theories of one man, and that erroneous thinking about the Treaty of Versailles, as Professor Shotwell has shown in "What Germany Forgot", is not a harmless thing.

4. That it is dangerous to confuse tolerance of persons with tolerance of falsehoods and that the principle of freedom even of false thought and speech is not to be construed as imposing silence on those who would answer falsehood with truth.

5. That true education of the minds of individuals and of nations and of the adult mind must be undertaken and adequately and persistently carried through and that such education calls for more unity of social and religious faith than we possess today—namely, for the whole Biblical faith.

6. That all negligence of duty entails, in the end, costs far in excess of any sacrifice which the fulfillment of duty could have invalued.

7. That our present, immediate duty is to destroy utterly the falsehoods of totalitarian tyranny and to proclaim and assure "liberty throughout the world unto all the inhabitants thereof."

These are some of the lessons America needs to learn and cannot learn too soon.

A Time for Penitence

By Israel Goldstein
President, Synagogue Council of America

THE ten years of Hitlerism will be known as the
decade that shook and shocked civilization. Most
shocking of all is the thought that Hitler almost suc-
ceeded. Future generations of mankind will tremble
to think that only by a hair's breadth did civilization
survive. June 1940, when France fell and England
stood alone, was the precariously balanced date. One
understands now what the Rabbis meant when they
said that "heaven and hell are separated by no more
than a hair's breadth."

Hindsight makes obvious what foresight should have
previsaged, that Hitler's attack upon the Jewish people and Judaism was but a prelude to the universal
melodrama. If the nations now united in war against
Hitler would have united ten or nine or even five years
ago to restrain the madman of Europe, untold millions
of human lives and untold billions of wealth would
have been spared.

The tenth anniversary of Hitlerism is a time for
contrition and penitence. This tragic decade has been
a man-made affliction.

Thank God, the all-but resistless tide of villainy is
being resisted at last, and being turned back upon
itself. Before another anniversary of Hitlerism will
have arrived, it will become a byword of dismal failure.

How many Jews in Europe will live to see that day? Apprehension gnaws at the heart. With prayer we turn toward the future.

Whatever the price may yet have to be, we know that "My Redeemer liveth". Mankind will be redeemed from the snare of the fowler. It will be established as a warning for the future that as sure as there is a God, tyranny is doomed to destruction. This, the fundamental premise and promise of Religion, is being vindicated by Hitler's doom. Having challenged Religion, and having sought to exterminate the carriers of Religion, Catholic, Protestant and Jew, he will perish by that challenge.

One hears reparations spoken of these days, proposals that Jewish property which has been robbed be restored to its rightful owners. Millions of martyred Jews, alas, will not be alive to receive restoration. Life cannot be restored to them. There is, however, one collective Jewish restoration which can be made, the restoration of the Jewish people to Eretz Israel and the restoration of Eretz Israel to the Jewish people. Let that be the charge upon the conscience of the United Nations and their atonement for the sins of omission which they have committed in Hitler's decade.

Worse Things Than War

By Father Nicholas Higgins

THE Tenth Anniversary of Nazism! The Tenth Anniversary of injustice, persecution, cruelty, barbarism, confiscation of property and belongings, of confinement in the ghetto or concentration camp, or banishment from one's native land; The Tenth Anniversary of malice with its attempts to destroy the Christian religion, and trumped up charges against its ministers, and the spoliation of the Church's goods; The Tenth Anniversary of scheming to defile youth, and to produce by education but a lot of clever young devils; The Tenth Anniversary of depriving man of his inherent rights—freedom to walk over the earth, freedom of conscience, freedom of religion, freedom of speech, freedom to attain the fruit of one's labors; The Tenth Anniversary of the ideology that man was made for the State, not the State for the man.

Linked with such an anniversary is the secret and feverish preparation by the Nazi gangsters for a fiendish war in which they have deserted all honor and chivalry and perpetrated all kinds of atrocities; sinking ships without warning, lying to lay the crime elsewhere, firing upon helpless survivors in the life-boats, not giving them a dog's chance or even a rat's chance; bombing open cities, sometimes to terrorize the people, sometimes in mad revenge, machine-gunning civilians in the streets. Bound up with this month ten years ago is a story of premediated cruelty, bullying, savagery, atrocity, and the fallacy that might is right.

But—But—there will soon be an end to such anniversaries. Already the handwriting is on the wall. Nazism will perish as every evil perishes and by its own hand. It has said, "Might is right" So be it. The might of the United Nations is now prevailing. Very different is the story now from what it was one year ago; still more different from what it was two years ago; more different again from what it was three years ago. Soon, if the names of Hitler and Goebbels and Goering and Schmitt, and those identified with Gestapo or "Clever Young Devils" are ever mentioned, they will be as a warning that injustice and bullying and cruelty bring their own punishment.

And soon we will celebrate truly joyous anniversaries, when we will recall wonderful sacrifices made by the peoples of many lands that liberty might not perish, we will sing of heroes and martyrs who welcome death before dishonor, we will praise our women and children for never faltering when the skies rained murder; we will glorify the splendid young men who battled by day and night against tremendous odds, and who merited the thankfulness of a great statesman who never feared to face facts and to utter truth, "Never before in the history of men have so many owed so much to so few;" we will reverence all those who lived and fought; perhaps died for "government of the people, by the people, for the people." Soon the bells of victory will ring out, and their message will be that good has triumphed over evil, justice over injustice, right over wrong, love over hatred, the powers of light over the powers of darkness.

In years to come mothers will tell their children how there once roamed the earth, a monster, called Nazism, destroying for destroying's sake, killing for killing's sake and how it was short-lived because men and women, although they hated war, knew that there could be worse things than war. And those worse things were tyranny and slavery under those deluded mortals who boasted of a purer blood and a superior race.

The children will wonder how in a free and beautiful world there could have arisen such a monster.

Crime Begets Crime

By Congressman Samuel Dickstein

On January 30 of this year, there will occur the tenth anniversary of the assumption of power, by the man who, more than anyone else, is responsible for the present world upheaval, and destruction of everything we hold dear and sacred.

On that fateful January 30, 1933, not many of us knew or suspected that a whole decade would pass before the combined power of the civilized world would be fighting to put an end to this nefarious rule of Hitler. No one took him seriously. The world at large was not particularly interested, because the world at large did not care, believing as they did, that Hitler's wrath was only directed against the Jewish people, and that there was no desire on his part to destroy the liberties of the whole world.

Hitler played his cards very shrewdly. His first speech to the German Reichstag was a plea for peace. Then there began that never ending race for rearmament and the creation of destructive weapons of war. When Hitler felt that he could dare the world he reoccupied the Rhineland, restored compulsory military service in Germany, killed the Austrian Chancellor and then, "purged" his own followers. In a short time, Hitler began the mastery of Central Europe, and everywhere his aggression became more pronounced and his mastery ever more all inclusive.

By 1938 Hitler felt that the Western democracies

had no power or desire to resist his encroachments. He amputated Czechoslovakia, annexed Austria, and finally declared war to the death on all that was civilized and cultured on the European continent.

There is an old saying that crime begets crime and Hitler's march across the continent of Europe resulted in complete destruction of the independence of many historic nations and peoples.

Since 1939 the whole world has been gradually engulfed in this titanic struggle for survival.

The Jewish people, who first felt the brunt of Hitler's enmity, have been particularly marked by him for destruction, and it was Hitler's policy to exterminate the Jewish race wherever his legions have marched. Poland has become the vast graveyard of millions of people, who are faced with complete extermination and extinction.

The world stands aghast at the enormity of Hitler's brutality and at the return to conditions which bring us back to the cruelties of the dark ages. But Hitler's crimes have finally brought enraged mankind to the point where the rest of the world has banded itself together to bring an end to this series of barbarities.

Since December 7, 1941, this country has pledged all of its resources and its vast man power to the task of seeing to it that these crimes shall never again plague mankind.

I hail the policy of your paper, which seeks to bring annually, a complete picture of Hitlerism, to the American public to the end that we become acquainted with what it stands for and its real aims and purposes. Let us hope that the next issue devoted to a discussion of Hitlerism will contain these welcome words, "Hitler and Hitlerism have perished."

Massacre of Mankind

By Emil Lengyel

THE Nazis celebrate the tenth anniversary of their coming into power by massacring millions of non-combatants. That is in character with their philosophy, which is a religion of murder.

Hitler has been compared to Genghis Kahn and also to the cannibals of the jungles. But Genghis Khan was a humanitarian in comparison with Hitler, because he killed merely as part of his military strategy. The Nazis, on the other hand, are killers not only for military reasons but because murder is their way of "life."

It was the custom of the jungle cannibals in the past to offer human lives on the funeral pyres of their chieftains. The Nazis are doing exactly the same. Since they do not seem to be strong enough to kill their enemies in combat, they massacre the non-combatants, offering them to the blood-thirsty gods of the Teutonic Valhalla on Nazi funeral pyres. But they are far more efficient and thorough than the black jungle people ever were. Thus they demonstrate Nordic superiority.

For the last ten years the Nazis have filled the

world's ears with their clamor for what they call a living space, *"Lebensraum."* Now there can be no doubt in any mind that their *"Lebensraum"* is the *"Todesraum"* of all the rest of the earth,—their living space is the mass grave of civilized humanity. At any rate, it would be if they had their way, but they are not having it. This is clear on the tenth anniversary of the assumption of power by organized terror.

Against Christian Conscience

By Father William C. Kernan

I DO not think that anti-Semitism is a crime which concerns only the Jews. I think that it is a crime which concerns all mankind, but more particularly Christians than any other people. It should be clear to Christians that the inhuman treatment by the Nazis of men who are Jews is the best evidence they need to prove that Hitler's plan is to remove from the face of the earth not only the Jews, but everything that the people of Palestine have given to the world—the knowledge of God, and the moral law, and the Christian religion.

Developments in occupied Europe certainly go far beyond merely suggesting that this is so, and if there is a man anywhere in America who still doubts that Nazism is the sworn enemy of Christianity let him ponder seriously the new decree of the German Government in Poland concerning the Church there. This decree, reported in a recent issue of *Christianity and Crisis*, sets up two divisions of the Church, one of which is for Germans, the other for Poles.

Thus, the Nazi theory of racial division is introduced into the Church of Christ where, of all places on this earth, it does not belong. It was no less an authority than St. Paul who wrote that "as many of you as have been baptized into Christ have put on Christ. There is neither Jew nor Greek, there is neither bond nor free, there is neither male nor female:

for ye are all one in Christ Jesus" (Galatians 3:27-28). This is the Christian answer to the Nazi pretentions to racial superiority and, in disregarding it, the Nazis compel Christians to act contrary to a basic tenet of the Christian religion.

With respect to the Jews the Nazi defiance of Christianity has gone even further. Both Protestants and Catholics in Holland are fully aware of this. In a recent protest against abuse of the Jews they expressed themselves as previously shocked by the treatment accorded the Jews in Holland, and filled with horror at "the new measures through which men, women, children and whole families are sent away to the territory of the German Reich and its dependencies."

The Dutch Christians saw in the suffering thus inflicted upon the Jews an offense against the Christian conscience and a "conflict between these measures and God's claims of justice and mercy." But they also took cognizance of the incontestable fact that by their actions the Nazis were excluding Jewish Christians "from participation in the life of the Church"—a direct defiance of the Christian principle that in the Church of Christ a new unity is created from which neither Jews nor Gentiles may be excluded. It is ironical to observe that had the Nazi doctrine of excluding Jews prevailed in the first Christian century not one of the Apostles would have been permitted to have become a member of the Church, for they were all Jews.

If Christianity is not for all men it ceases to be a universal religion, which means that it ceases to be Christianity. It becomes something else—a national cult or an instrument of the State—something that the

Nazis want to make it. Christians cannot have it both ways. But, if Christians want the Christianity of Christ and the Church of Christ they will have to make up their minds to rise in all their strength against Nazism, in America and elsewhere, or else reconcile themselves to the persecution of Christians by the same moral perverts who now plan to exterminate the Jews. For, "we are all Abraham's children, we are all spiritually Semites."

The Next Ten Years

By Lewis Gannett

I DON'T think more words are needed to convince the American people that it must battle on until the curse of Hitlerism is lifted from mankind. The only thing the people of America are afraid of today is words. They are tired of words, suspicious of words, healthily skeptical of words. Perhaps, some times, too skeptical of words.

For we need words, not so much to convince the people that Hitler is foul—ask the boys in the army about that, and the girls they left behind, and you won't find much skepticism as to that first goal. The uncertain morale of a year and a half ago is vanished. The danger today is not that we shall falter short of victory, but that we shall not know how to make military victory into something permanent. We need words for discussion of the long road that will lie beyond the armistice. The really dangerous isolationism of today is post-war isolationism.

There we need rather calm, skeptical words than eloquent words. None of us can afford to be too sure of procedure. The men who framed the Treaty of Versailles were neither fools nor criminals. They did their best, amid a conflict of opinions as to what was best. It wasn't good enough—partly because the leaders did not know enough to do a good enough job, partly because the peoples back home—in France and

England and America—were not prepared to support even that not-good-enough best. Eloquence won't help today. Calm discussion may. But the people will continue healthily skeptical of large, glib words.

So I am a little sorry that OPINION devotes its special issue to "Ten Years of Hitlerism"—to the past. The ten years after the signing at Versailles were devoted to meditating on the past, and to an effort to "return to normalcy"—and they led to the Great Collapse of 1929. Devote your next issue to the Ten Years After Hitler—and remember that Versailles didn't work.

Hitlerism Versus Brotherhood

By Rudolph I. Coffee
President, National Chaplains Association

TEN years ago, a diabolical creed arose in Germany. It was so unbelievably brutal and breathing hatred against all non-Aryans, that Americans paid little attention to it. The few who criticized its infamy were promptly called war-mongers. Not until hundreds of thousands of Jews had been exiled or murdered, not until government after government in Europe had been overthrown, followed by the bestial attack on Pearl Harbor, did liberty-loving people see Hitler in his true light.

Today, the civilized world is fighting magnificently to preserve the moral and ethical gains of the past million years. The United Nations realize that Hitler cannot be allowed to exterminate the Jews and become a world conqueror. To prevent that colossal catastrophe, the vast resources of civilized man are now co-operating to overthrow Hitlerism and to prevent for all times another Hitler from endangering the peace of the world.

But a military victory will not be enough. The United Nations, victorious in war, must continue in order to preserve the peace. A police force, controlling the sea, air and land will deny to any man or group the right to challenge the peace of this globe. The United States, a loyal partner among the United

Nations in war, will remain a vital force in its post-war operations.

It is unthinkable that the isolationists will again cause us to lose the peace as in 1919. Millions of Americans now realize that only by our union with other nations, can a third world war be prevented.

Nor will a military victory, followed by a military peace, suffice. Universal peace must be founded not on the sword but on brotherly love. The world's greatest command is still "Love thy neighbor". Catholic, Jewish and Protestant leaders have warmly endorsed plans for universal peace as the cornerstone of the world we want to live in. One additional step is essential—the desire for religious people to work together for this new world order. Why not? Catholics, Jews and Protestants worship the same God and uphold the same ideals.

Why cannot religious leaders unite when lay groups are standing together against the common foe—dictatorship? All the governments in the Americas, with one exception, and all the English-speaking peoples have joined hands. Oceans no longer divide. The world is growing smaller and man is growing larger, spiritually. All these fine forces are joined in the resolve to build the new social order, according to the blue print of the Hebraic vision, where "They shall dwell every man under his own vine and fig tree, with none to make them afraid". Such a universe will end the exile of the wandering Jew.

Resurrection for Mankind

By Estelle M. Sternberger

I T seems like a nightmare as we look back upon these
ten years of Nazism. When it was on its way to power,
people refused to believe that any combination of men
would dare carry out the threats implicit in the announced credo of Nazism. Now that Nazism has had
the opportunity to make its creed effective, some men
and women in various parts of the world still remain
sceptical toward the story charged against Nazism.
It is the story of hate elevated to a "religion," of murder and of pillage.

In this hour of review in which the editors of OPINION
have invited us to participate, I cannot refrain from re-
calling that many of the world's ablest interpreters of
the Bible in this recent century, came from Germany.
The Bible was a mine in which a considerable number
of Germans went digging for the secrets of spirituality
and civilization. Theology, Archaeology, Egyptology,
Assyriology and other branches of human interest
found food for thought and adventure in the pages of
the Bible that Hitler rejects.

It was because Germany was sensitive to the idealism
of the Bible that it made it the foundation stone of
many cultural and scientific achievement. That
idealism was too recently present in Germany for us
to draw a curtain over it. The roots of that idealism
must still be there no matter how heavy the blanket of
suppression thrown over them by Hitler. Those roots

must inevitably sprout forth as soon as the restraining blanket of Hitlerism is removed.

There is one certainty on the horizon of mankind: that Hitler will pass into the eternal shadows. History will never describe him as one of humanity's heroes, for he has lacked the sense of humanity. Only madmen may read the records of today, at some future date, and try to emulate what he did. But the great mass of human beings will use his name as a synonym for Attila and the Vandals.

As we face the judgments of history, we must not soothe ourselves with the thought that Hitler will fare badly at the bar of world opinion. We owe a debt to the generations of tomorrow and to our own that we ought to begin discharging today. We must accept a spiritual discipline that draws its rules from the code of universal brotherhood under God. We must be as eager to carry its requirements into effect as we are to perform the requirements of our wartime rationing and other boards. We must rise to the fact that discipline to carry us through a world crisis is something beyond the limitation of meat and gasoline consumption.

If we deplore the course of events that tore thousands and millions of Germans away from the spiritual pages of the Bible, we ought to reflect on the distance that separates us from the laws of love and peace that Israel's prophets and Jesus and his disciples taught men on the hillsides and in the valleys of the Palestine that gave them birth. This war will have been a fruitless war if its victory should seek only to return Germans to the influence of the Bible. We too must accept the Bible. We must walk humbly with God and be confident that we are performing his will among the men near us.

No Hitler could ever again rise anywhere if we in this generation, and the generations after us, make brotherhood come true in every community of America and in every hamlet of civilization. Hitler worked with a furious speed these ten years to perform his program of destruction. We must progress spiritually more speedily than ever before, if we hope to overcome the full extent of his destruction and to give mankind an eternal resurrection.

Atrocities and Punishment
By Congressman Emanuel Celler

THE number of Jewish victims deported or perished since 1939 in Axis-controlled Europe now reaches the appalling figure of 2,000,000. 5,000,000 are in danger of extermination. Hitler and his jackals have vowed to make Europe Judenrein. Not since the days of Genghis Khan or Attila have we witnessed such horrors of mass torture and murder.

"The righteous shall rejoice when he seeth the vengeance: He shall wash his feet in the blood of the wicked." (Psalms, 58) The Allied Nations must follow this Biblical admonition. We must beware the pitfalls of the last World War.

When Kaiser Wilhelm, the Crown Prince, Count Bismarck and Field Marshals Hindenberg and Ludendorff were not brought to justice, the Government of Holland refused to allow, for example, any extradition. Indictments were drawn against 900 murderers, but, sad to relate, only twelve were actually tried and six convicted. The farce continued in the imposition of two four year sentences of imprisonment for two naval officers (the heaviest punishment accorded) and for the others, six months in jail. Add the cynical note that the two lieutenants somehow contrived to escape to a comfortable exile, and the puny efforts of the allied powers to serve the ends of justice stand forth as a sorry tale of diplomatic deceit and dishonesty. It was a pathetic procedure and we must not allow a repetition.

We might well follow the pattern of Russia. They have not waited until the end of the war to try these mongrels. They have set up an "Extraordinary State Commission" to investigate now, not later, the atrocities, the damage to property, to assess now, not later, the amount of reparation, to identify now, not later, the guilty. Very significantly, the chairmanship is held by a Trade Union leader and includes among its members a brain surgeon, a historian, a distinguished writer and a woman pilot.

I shall offer a bill in Congress to set up such a commission to be composed primarily of civilians with few, if any, diplomats. Women and labor shall play an appropriate part in its deliberations. They shall not wait until victory is achieved to point the avenging finger and to demand an "eye for an eye and a tooth for a tooth."

A Trail of Degeneration

By Eduard C. Lindeman

I have had the unhappy experience of living in Italy when Fascism came to that land and in Germany when Hitler came to power. I saw what could happen to human beings once this disease had begun its fateful course. I saw fine, liberal, tolerant persons transformed almost over night into bigoted, fanatical hateful beings. So, I became an anti-Fascist at the very beginning because it came to me as a sharp realization that this was a disease which anybody might "catch" if circumstances were favorable.

At the end of a decade of this madness in Germany one may begin to make an appraisal. Now and then I encounter people who say in an apologetic manner, "yes, but after all Hitler has done some good things for Germany and for the World." Whoever says this to me must place his "good" beside my audit of evils.

Since Hitler began his program of systematized hate, over 16,000,000 young men of Europe have lost their lives in warfare;

Between four and six million human beings have been forcefully torn from their homelands, "kidnapped" and forced to live elsewhere;

Over 2,000,000 Jews have been massacred;

Precious libraries in occupied countries have been destroyed;

The cultured leadership in occupied countries has been liquidated.

I need not compile a fuller list. It is already evident that no man of history has left in his wake so great a trail of death and degeneration. The citizen of this nation who does not yet realize the insidiousness of this Fascist disease, its inner evil, must be blind indeed. Those of us who do feel this realization can only resolve that if it is in our power this disease shall never come to us; but this resolve will have meaning only if we at the same moment determine to give all possible aid in rotting it out of the soil of Europe.

National Insanity

By Leverett Saltonstall
Governor of Massachusetts

I т is ten years now since Adolf Hitler rose to power. In this decade he has turned the clock back and halted the progress of civilization. His ruthless persecution of men of all faiths, his destruction of the labor union movement in Germany and his utter disregard for the principles of liberty, justice and equality, have plunged this world into the most horrible war in its history. Under Hitler the Nazi government has sought to create a world in which the Germans would be masters and the rest of the world slaves. As Hitler himself said: "There will be a Herren-Class. And there will be the great mass. Beneath them there will still be the class of subject alien races; we need not hesitate to call them the modern slave class." It is against this philosophy—the complete repudiation of the dignity of the individual man—that the United Nations are today warring. We are fighting for a world in which there will be freedom of worship, freedom of press, freedom of expression, and where all men will have the right to live as free men.

In every action that Hitler and the Nazi government have taken they have repudiated these great principles. Churchmen — Catholics, Protestants and Jews — have been imprisoned because they would not bow to Nazism.

Leaders of capital and labor have been destroyed unless they took instructions from Hitler's so-called "labor front." Women have been enslaved, disenfranchised, as the Nazis officially proclaimed a state policy that enshrined illegitimacy and destroyed all real family life.

That Hitler's persecution of the Jews—a part of his total war—should now culminate in a program of complete extermination is a logical development in the Nazi program. All the world views with horror this newest manifestation of national insanity. It is, of course, just one more step in the degradation of the German nation.

The record of a decade of Nazi horror and the prospect of future cruelties by an enraged Hitler, slowly but surely losing the war, should spur the people of the United Nations to greater efforts so that this war may be brought to a speedy and victorious conclusion. Only then, can we look to a world of the future when men of all faiths, of all nationalities, of all colors, shall enjoy their God-given right to live as free men.